My Friend Joe

Written and illustrated by Russell Ayto

Collins

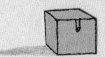

2

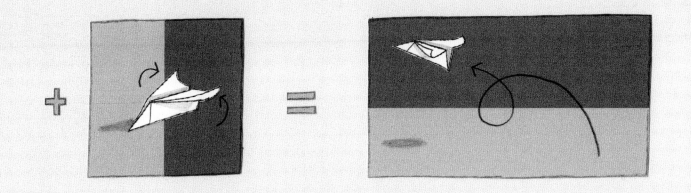

Making friends

Ideas for reading

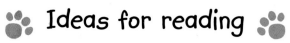

Written by Clare Dowdall, PhD
Lecturer and Primary Literacy Consultant

Reading objectives:
- demonstrate understanding when talking with others about what they have read

Communication and language objectives:
- listen to stories, accurately anticipating key events and respond to what they hear with relevant comments, questions or actions
- express themselves effectively, showing awareness of listeners' needs
- develop their own narratives and explanations by connecting ideas or events

Curriculum links: Personal, social and emotional development

Interest words: friend

Resources: paper, paper plane designs, pens or pencils for drawing

Build a context for reading

- Ask children to talk about what they do with their friends. Make a list of some things that friends do together.

- Look at the front and back covers. Read the title and blurb to the children, pointing to each word as you read.

- Using the illustration, discuss what is happening in the picture. Ask children to suggest what might happen to the children in the story. Use questions to support children's thinking and language, e.g. *Will the boys become friends?*

Understand and apply reading strategies

- Begin to look through the book together. Dwell on pp2–3. Give children time to look at the pictures and talk about what they can see.

- Model how to make meaning from the pictures by talking aloud, e.g. *I think that the dotted lines show that the boy is throwing a paper plane.*

- Help children to understand how to order the information in the pictures, page by page. Explain that on pp2–3, the events move down the page, and on pp4–5 the events move across the page.

- Continue to look through the book, encouraging children to share their ideas about what is happening in the pictures. Use questioning to help children think about what the characters are doing and how they are feeling. At the end of each double page, ask children to suggest what might happen next.